Citizenship:
Rights and Responsibilities

ROB MAURY

MAJOR AMERICAN IMMIGRATION

MASON CREST PUBLISHERS • PHILADELPHIA

In September 1984, nearly 10,000 people participated in one of the largest naturalization ceremonies in U.S. history at the Orange Bowl Stadium in Miami. Naturalization is the final step immigrants must take to become citizens of the United States.

Citizenship:
Rights and Responsibilities

ROB MAURY

MAJOR AMERICAN IMMIGRATION

MASON CREST PUBLISHERS • PHILADELPHIA

Mason Crest Publishers
370 Reed Road
Broomall PA 19008
www.masoncrest.com

Copyright © 2009 by Mason Crest Publishers. All rights reserved.
Printed and bound in Malaysia.

First printing

1 3 5 7 9 8 6 4 2

Library of Congress Cataloging-in-Publication Data

Maury, Rob.
  Citizenship : rights and responsibilities / Rob Maury.
      p. cm. — (Major American immigration)
  Includes index.
  ISBN 978-1-4222-0618-8 (hardcover)
  ISBN 978-1-4222-0685-0 (pbk.)
  1. United States—Emigration and immigration—History—Juvenile
literature. 2. Citizenship—United States—Juvenile literature. I. Title.
  JV6450.C664 2008
  323.6'50973—dc22
                                             2008028223

Table of Contents

MAJOR AMERICAN IMMIGRATION

America's Ethnic Heritage

Barry Moreno, librarian
Statue of Liberty/
Ellis Island National Monument

Ethnic diversity is one of the most striking characteristics of the American identity. In the United States the Bureau of the Census officially recognizes 122 different ethnic groups. North America's population had grown by leaps and bounds, starting with the American Indian tribes and nations—the continent's original people—and increasing with the arrival of the European colonial migrants who came to these shores during the 16th and 17th centuries. Since then, millions of immigrants have come to America from every corner of the world.

But the passage of generations and the great distance of America from the "Old World"—Europe, Africa, and Asia—has in some cases separated immigrant peoples from their roots. The struggle to succeed in America made it easy to forget past traditions. Further, the American spirit of freedom, individualism, and equality gave Americans a perspective quite different from the view of life shared by residents of the Old World.

Immigrants of the 19th and 20th centuries recognized this at once. Many tried to "Americanize" themselves by tossing away their peasant clothes and dressing American-style even before reaching their new homes in the cities or the countryside of America. It was not so easy to become part of America's culture, however. For many immigrants, learning English was quite a hurdle. In fact, most older immigrants clung to the old ways, preferring to speak their native languages and follow their familiar customs and traditions. This was easy to do when ethnic neighborhoods abounded in large North American cities like New York, Montreal, Philadelphia, Chicago, Toronto, Boston, Cleveland, St. Louis, New Orleans and San Francisco. In rural areas, farm families—many of them Scandinavian, German, or Czech—established their own tightly knit communities. Thus foreign languages and dialects, religious beliefs, Old World customs, and certain class distinctions flourished.

The most striking changes occurred among the children of immigrants, whose hopes and dreams were different from those of their parents. They began breaking away from the Old World customs, perhaps as a reaction to the embarrassment of being labeled "foreigner." They badly wanted to be Americans, and assimilated more easily than their parents and grandparents. They learned to speak English without a foreign accent, to dress and act like other Americans. The assimilation of the children of immigrants was encouraged by social contact—games, schools, jobs, and military service—which further broke down the barriers between immigrant groups and hastened the process of Americanization. Along the way, many family traditions were lost or abandoned.

Today, the pride that Americans have in their ethnic roots is one of the abiding strengths of both the United States and Canada. It shows that the theory which called America a "melting pot" of the world's people was never really true. The thought that a single "American" would emerge from the combination of these peoples has never happened, for Americans have grown more reluctant than ever before to forget the struggles of their ethnic forefathers. The growth of cultural studies and genealogical research indicates that Americans are anxious not to entirely lose this identity, whether it is English, French, Chinese, African, Mexican, or some other group. There is an interest in tracing back the family line as far as records or memory will take them. In a sense, this has made Americans a divided people; proud to be Americans, but proud also of their ethnic roots.

As a result, many Americans have welcomed a new identity, that of the hyphenated American. This unique description has grown in usage over the years and continues to grow as more Americans recognize the importance of family heritage. In the end, this is an appreciation of America's great cultural heritage and its richness of its variety.

Personal Stories of United States Immigration

1

Many people come to America looking for a better life, but not every person's experiences are pleasant.

In 1977, Donna was 13 and swimming in the waters surrounding her island home, Jamaica. Life was warm under the tropical sun, and Donna playing on the beach with her two brothers, ages 15 and three. She went to school like most kids her age. However, not many kids could pick and eat mangos off a tree on their way home. One morning, her mother woke her up, saying, "Get dressed. We're leaving for America."

Donna's parents wanted freedom from political **persecution**. Jamaica's newly appointed prime minister had **allied** himself with Cuba's Communist leader Fidel Castro. That morning, Donna and her

President George W. Bush poses with new American citizens after a swearing-in ceremony on Ellis Island. According to government statistics, Each year about 1 million immigrants become U.S. citizens.

family boarded a plane headed for Miami, Florida, with one suitcase each and $50. They were lucky because many people didn't make it past the airport guards. Donna and her family had to pretend they were only leaving to visit America.

In Miami, Donna and her brothers stayed with friends while her parents went further north to Baltimore, Maryland. Terrified of being sent back to Jamaica, Donna and her brothers stayed inside. The carefree girl who once skipped on the wide, open beach now felt trapped, frightened, and alone.

Once her parents were settled and employed, they sent for the children. For the second time in her life, Donna hopped on a plane headed for a place unknown to her. When she landed in Baltimore, it was the middle of winter—a winter with heavy snowfall. Wearing sandals and no coats, Donna and her brothers were not prepared for the freezing temperatures of the Baltimore winters. Living with snow was something that had never occurred to Donna. She was used to tropical weather and sandy beaches.

Donna's parents had found a place for her and her brothers to live, but it wasn't with them. For three months, the children lived in one room in a townhouse in downtown Baltimore. Scared, Donna anxiously waited for the day her family would be together again. The only thing available for Donna and her older brother to do was take care of their younger brother.

The day finally came when Donna's family was together again. For the third time in less than a year, her life changed once more. She was now living in Baltimore, going to an American school, and dreaming of her former tropical-paradise home.

Years later, her parents decided to become ***naturalized*** United States citizens. Today, they raise foster children as a way to say

GLORIA ESTEFAN

Most immigrants come to the United States seeking the "American Dream," and Gloria Estefan was no different. Gloria Fajardo (Estefan is her married name) was born in Havana, Cuba, in 1957. Fidel Castro's policies forced Gloria and her family to migrate to the United States in 1959. Her father served with the United States Army as a soldier in Vietnam. After Vietnam, he developed *multiple sclerosis*. As the oldest daughter, Gloria took care of him and her younger sister while her mother worked to support the family. Her music career was launched while she attended the University of Miami. There she joined a band called The Miami Sound Machine. Since then, she has won many awards, including several Grammys. In addition to continuing her successful music career she is also an outspoken supporter of a free Cuba.

HAKEEM OLAJUWON

Hakeem Olajuwon's coming-to-America story started on the basketball court. He was born in 1963 in Lagos, Nigeria. As a boy, he went to school (where he learned French and four dialects of the Nigerian language) and loved to play soccer and handball. As a teen, he started playing basketball. Within weeks, thanks to his height and skill, he made the Nigerian national team. An American coach traveling in Nigeria was so overwhelmed by his talent that he searched for a college in the United States that would offer Hakeem a scholarship.

Hakeem came to the United States for a college education and a chance to play basketball at the University of Houston. He remembers his first stop in the United States as being very cold. His first stop, like many coming to the United States, was in New York.

Hakeem's decision to become a United States citizen in 1993 was a difficult one. However, he felt a debt of gratitude to the country that had given so much to him, including an education, a career as a professional basketball player, and a family.

thanks to the country that fostered their children. After becoming a naturalized United States citizen, her older brother joined the United States Marine Corps. Her younger brother attended college.

Donna's decision to become a naturalized American citizen didn't come as easy for her as it had for her parents. She was an adult when her parents became citizens, leaving it up to her to decide if she wanted to give up her Jamaican citizenship. She still dreamed of her tropical-paradise home. Today, she still lives in Baltimore, but now with her husband and three young children. It was having children that made her decide to become a United States citizen. They represented the first generation of Jamaican-American, natural-born United States citizens in Donna's family. As the only member of her family not a United States citizen, being sent back to Jamaica finally became a real terror for her.

The test wasn't as hard for her as it might have been for other immigrants because Donna had spent all her high school years in the United States. It did take years, however, to get through each step leading up to the day she finally took the oath.

Citizenship has proven to be beneficial. Now Donna can help determine what happens in her community, her children's schools, and who represents her in government by voting. She can visit Jamaica, lie on its sunny beaches, and swim in its blue water without fear of having to immediately leave with only a suitcase and $50. ✹

Benefits of U.S. Citizenship

The Constitution and laws of the United States give many rights to both citizens and non-citizens living in the United States. However, some rights are only for citizens, such as:

- Voting. Only U.S. citizens can vote in Federal elections. Most States also restrict the right to vote, in most elections, to U.S. citizens.

- Bringing family members to the United States. Citizens generally get priority when petitioning to bring family members permanently to this country.

- Obtaining citizenship for children born abroad. In most cases, a child born abroad to a U.S. citizen is automatically a U.S. citizen.

- Traveling with a U.S. passport. A U.S. passport allows you to get assistance from the U.S. government when overseas.

- Becoming eligible for Federal jobs. Most jobs with government agencies require U.S. citizenship.

- Becoming an elected official. Many elected offices in this country require U.S. citizenship.

The above list does not include all the benefits of citizenship, only some of the more important ones.

Responsibilities of U.S. Citizenship

To become a U.S. citizen you must take the Oath of Allegiance. The Oath includes several promises you make when you become a U.S. citizen, including promises to:

- Give up all prior allegiance to any other nation or sovereignty;
- Swear allegiance to the United States;
- Support and defend the Constitution and the laws of the United States; and
- Serve the country when required.

U.S. citizens have many responsibilities other than the ones mentioned in the Oath. Citizens have a responsibility to participate in the political process by registering and voting in elections. Serving on a jury is another responsibility of citizenship. Finally, America becomes stronger when all of its citizens respect the different opinions, cultures, ethnic groups, and religions found in this country. Tolerance for differences is also a responsibility of citizenship.

Source: U.S. Citizenship and Immigration Services, *A Guide to Naturalization*, http://www.uscis.gov/files/article/M-476.pdf.

More than 12 million immigrants passed through the immigration center at Ellis Island before the station was closed in 1954. The buildings have been turned into a museum of immigration history, where visitors to the island can learn about the immigration experience.

2 History of United States Immigration

The United States started as a nation of immigrants, and throughout the centuries the nation has grown and developed because of immigrants. Most immigrants come to the United States for the chance to find better jobs, thus paving the way to a better life for their families. Immigrants have also come to the United States for other reasons, such as religious or political freedom.

In many cities in the United States, it is possible to drive from one end of the city to the other and pass many neighborhoods that embrace a culture from another country. All those culturally enhanced neighborhoods existing together in one city are what make this country a diverse and unique community.

Around A.D. 1000, Viking explorer Leif Eriksson sailed across the Atlantic and landed in Newfoundland, where he established a short-lived settlement. However, Europeans did not really begin to settle in North America until after Christopher Columbus's voyages. Looking for a westward route to Asia, Columbus sailed into the Caribbean in 1492, landing on several islands. Columbus made four voyages, during which he discovered and named many Caribbean islands and sailed along much of South America's east coast.

Columbus never admitted that he had not found Asia. It was another explorer, Amerigo Vespucci, who declared that he had found a "New World" after exploring Brazil's east coast in 1501. The new continents would eventually be named for Vespucci.

The discovery of this New World launched a major migration of Europeans into America. During the 1520s and 1530s, the Spanish made several attempts to settle in North America. In 1565, Spain established the first permanent European colony in North America at St. Augustine, Florida. By 1598, Spanish settlers had moved as far west as New Mexico.

France followed Spain to North America. In 1534 Jacques Cartier explored Newfoundland and the Gulf of St. Lawrence, claiming this territory for France. The French eventually settled in Acadia (Nova

Settlers trade with Indians at Jamestown, the first permanent English settlement in North America.

The Pilgrims established their colony as a place where they could practice their religion freely.

Scotia) in 1604 and Quebec in 1608. From there, they moved south into central North America, establishing New Orleans in 1718.

In 1607, three English ships landed in Virginia, where they established Jamestown, the first permanent English colony. Other English settlements would soon follow. In 1620 the Pilgrims crossed the Atlantic on their small ship *Mayflower*, founding the Plymouth colony in the area that became known as New England. A few years later, another English group, the Puritans, settled on the shores of Massachusetts Bay. In 1682, William Penn founded the colony of Pennsylvania. Although Penn was an English gentleman, he invited people from all countries— particularly Germans—to settle in his new colony.

Other European countries also established colonies in the New World during the 17th century. Swedes established New Sweden in 1638 in present-day Delaware. The Dutch founded the New Netherlands colony in 1614, and within it grew the town of New Amsterdam in 1626. In 1654, a group of Jewish settlers arrived at New Amsterdam. The Dutch eventually gained control of New Sweden. Later, the English took over the Dutch colony, renaming the city New York.

The African migration to North America was unlike any other. Africans were kidnapped from their homes and forced to work and live in North America. Portuguese slavers had been bringing African slaves to the Spanish and Portuguese colonies in South America and the Caribbean since the 1500s. In 1619 at Jamestown, the first slaves were sold in North America.

Immigration to North America continued throughout the 18th century, although the rate of new arrivals slowed during the American Revolution

African slaves work in a field of sugar cane. By 1790, about 700,000 African-American slaves lived in the United States.

(1775-1783). That war between Great Britain and 13 of its North American colonies ended with the independence of a new nation: the United States.

Once the war ended, people continued to come to North America. During the 1780s, thousands of Scottish immigrants arrived in America. In the 1790s, thousands of French people fled the bloody excesses of the French Revolution for the United States. By the time the second U.S. census was taken in 1800, the United States had a population of 5.3 million people.

The continued influx of people led the U.S. government to begin passing laws related to citizenship and immigration. In 1790, Congress passed an act that required newcomers to America to live in the United States for two years before they could qualify for citizenship. Five years later, Congress raised this time period to five years. Then, in 1798, Congress raised the time period to 14 years with the passage of the Alien and Sedition Acts.

During the 1840s, million of new immigrants arrived in North America. Most were from Ireland, Germany, and England. Germans came to avoid wars in their homeland, while the Irish came to America because of a potato *famine* on their island. In the West, Chinese immigrants begin arriving around 1848. They were hired as laborers on railroads and other major building projects. Between 1840 and 1880, about 37 million people came to North America.

Immigration helped the United States grow and prosper. However, some people feared that immigrants would take over jobs, or would

This advertisement for an anti-immigrant publication, circa 1852, portrays Irish immigrants as unkempt ruffians.

impose their foreign beliefs and values on American society. They wanted laws that would stop foreigners from coming to the United States. The government complied.

In 1882, Congress halted immigration from China by passing the Chinese Exclusion Act. Other laws were passed that prevented the immigration of criminals, people with diseases, and people likely to be dependent on public assistance. The Alien Contract Labor Laws of 1885 prohibited immigrants from entering the country to work under contracts made before they arrived. Exceptions were made for entertainers, educators, ministers, servants, and some skilled workers.

In 1891, Congress created the Immigration and Naturalization Service (INS) to administer federal laws relating to the admission, exclusion, and *deportation* of immigrants. The Immigration and Naturalization Service was also given the duty of lawfully naturalizing immigrants. The gateway to America, Ellis Island in New York Harbor, opened in 1892 and served as the Immigration and Naturalization Service's primary immigrant-screening station until it was closed in 1954.

From 1900 to the 1920s, about 10 million people immigrated to the United States. Many were from places like Japan, Italy, and eastern Europe. Their arrival in large numbers led to renewed calls for immigration limits. In 1907, the United States made an agreement with the Japanese government to prevent Japanese workers from coming to the United States. The Immigration Act of 1917 limited the areas of the world from which people were allowed to immigrate. In 1921, Congress enacted a *quota* system, limiting the number of immigrants allowed

This political cartoon from 1921 shows Uncle Sam slowing the rush of European immigrants to a trickle.

in the country each year. In 1924, Congress passed another immigration act, which reduced the number of immigrants allowed each year even further.

During the 1940s, Congress began to lift immigration *bans*. The War Brides Act of 1945 allowed entry to foreign women who had married U.S. soldiers or sailors serving overseas during World War II. The Displaced Persons Acts of 1948 and 1950, as well as the Refugee Relief Act of 1953, ushered in half a million people escaping the devastation of Europe or Communist persecution. Also in the 1950s, Mexican immigration numbers rose as people there fled poverty and a strict *dictatorship*.

This photo shows cars lined up south of the Mexican border, waiting to pass through a checkpoint and enter the United States. Each year, about 150,000 Mexican immigrants become citizens of the United States.

In 1965, the Immigration and Nationality Act set a new direction for U.S. immigration policy. Previously, the quota systems had ensured that most immigrants to America came from western Europe. The new law made it possible for people from all countries to come to America. Soon, there was a boom in immigration from Asia, Africa, and South and Central America.

In 1978, the Immigration and Nationality Act was amended. The new law set an annual worldwide limit of 290,000 immigrant *visas*, with a maximum of 20,000 for each country. The Refugee Act of 1980 reduced the worldwide quota to 270,000 and established a limit of 50,000 for refugees. Family members of people who had already immigrated to the United States were not subject to these quotas, however. As a result, by the 1990s the United States was admitting 1 million or more immigrants each year.

Along with this huge rise in legal immigration came concerns about increases in the number of undocumented, or illegal, immigrants entering the United States. In 1986, the Immigration Reform and Control Act penalized employers who hired illegal immigrants. In 1996, Congress made it easier to deport illegal immigrants by passing the Illegal Immigrant Reform and Immigration Responsibility Act.

After the September 11, 2001, terrorist attacks against the United States, new laws were passed to tighten U.S. borders. Despite these laws, by 2008 the U.S. Border Patrol estimated that 12 million illegal immigrants live in the United States. Three-quarters of illegal immigrants are from Mexico or Central America. ✺

STATUE OF LIBERTY

The Statue of Liberty (left) greeted many immigrants coming across the Atlantic Ocean in the early 1900s. The Statue of Liberty was a gift of friendship from France. Since 1886, Lady Liberty has stood tall (151 feet tall) on Liberty Island in New York Harbor near Ellis Island. In her right hand she holds high a torch representing liberty, and in her left a tablet with the date July 4, 1776 inscribed on it in roman numerals. The seven spikes of her crown represent the seven seas and the seven continents. There are 25 windows symbolizing the 25 gemstones of the earth. On the base of the statue is the poem "The New Colossus" by Emma Lazarus:

> *Not like the brazen giant of Greek fame*
> *With conquering limbs astride from land to land*
> *Here at our sea-washed, sunset gates shall stand*
> *A mighty woman with a torch, whose flame*
> *Is the imprisoned lightning, and her name*
> *Mother of Exiles. From her beacon-hand*
> *Glows worldwide welcome; her mild eyes command*
> *The air-bridged harbor that twin cities frame.*
> *"Give me your tired, your poor,*
> *Your huddled masses yearning to breathe free;*
> *The wretched refuse of your teeming shore,*
> *Send these, the homeless, tempest-tossed to me*
> *I lift my lamp beside the golden door!"*

The Statue of Liberty became a national monument symbolizing freedom in 1924.

3

Rights of United States Citizens

When an immigrant becomes a citizen of the United States, he or she gains all the rights and privileges of citizenship. These rights are spelled out in the U.S. Constitution, the foundation of all law and government in the United States.

On July 4, 1776, the 13 English colonies in North America declared their independence as a new nation with the document we call the Declaration of Independence. After defeating the British forces during the War for Independence, the new country—the United States of America—was governed by the Articles of Confederation. However, this system of government did not work very well. In 1787, American leaders decided to create a new system of government. The result of their work, the United States Constitution, went into effect in 1788.

The U.S. Constitution, the basis of government in the United States, has been in use for more than 200 years. It provides laws and guidelines for the government and explains the rights of U.S. citizens.

The Constitution set up a government with three branches: the legislative, the executive, and the judicial. A complex system of checks and balances was installed to ensure that all branches had equal power. One example of the checks and balances system is that when Congress (the House of Representatives and Senate) passes a law, the President can veto, or reject, the law, or the Supreme Court can determine that the law is **unconstitutional**—that is, it violates the U.S. Constitution.

The Constitution includes a preamble, followed by seven sections called articles. Article One of the Constitution deals with the legislative branch of the United States government—the House of Representatives and the Senate. This is the branch of government that is responsible for making the laws of the United States. Article One ensures that all citizens who pay taxes will have representation in government. A **census** is taken every 10 years to determine the nation's population. The number of representatives in the House of Representatives is determined by the number of people living in each state. Currently, there are 435 representatives, each of whom are elected to a two-year term. Every state is represented by two senators, each of whom serve six-year terms.

Article Two discusses the executive branch—the president and vice president. The president's duties include ensuring that the nation's laws are enforced and acting as commander-in-chief of all United States military forces. If the president is unable to fulfill his duties, the vice president assumes these responsibilities.

Article Three covers the judicial branch—the court system, including the Supreme Court. The Supreme Court's duties include reviewing legal decisions made by lower courts to determine whether they comply with the intent of the Constitution.

The United States Supreme Court building stands
in Washington, D.C. The Supreme Court is made up
of nine justices whose task is to interpret the U.S.
Constitution as it relates to the laws of the land.

Article Four keeps all the states on equal grounds. Article Five sets
the standards for ***amending*** the Constitution. Article Six proclaims the
Constitution as the supreme law of the land. Article Seven states that the
approval of nine states was needed for the Constitution to go into effect.

33

WASHINGTON, DISTRICT OF COLUMBIA

Named for George Washington and Christopher Columbus, Washington, D.C., was established as a federal territory in 1790 and became the new capital of the United States. Today, the city's population has grown to over half a million. The Home Rule Act of 1974 established local elections for the mayor and city council. However, the federal government still primarily governs Washington, D.C. In March 2000, city residents sought representation in Congress, but were denied by a panel of judges.

The Constitution was made so that it could be amended as needed. On September 25, 1789, Congress proposed 12 amendments, and on December 15, 1791, 10 went into effect. These amendments addressed concerns and lingering fears that people had about repressive government. The 10 amendments are called the Bill of Rights. They guarantee certain rights and privileges to all citizens of the United States.

The First Amendment guarantees the freedom of speech, press, and religion. This means that the government cannot prevent a person from speaking out, a newspaper from running an article critical of the government, or a person from worshipping as he or she chooses, as long as these things do not infringe on any other person's rights.

The Second Amendment gives citizens the right to bear arms. In other words, this amendment says that law-abiding citizens have the right to own guns. The level of gun control permitted under the Second Amendment is a heavily debated issue today.

The Third Amendment bans the housing of members of the military in civilian homes. During the Revolutionary War, English troops took over the homes of civilians, thus prompting the passage of this amendment.

The Fourth Amendment prevents illegal search and seizures. This means the police can not search or take away a person's property without reasonable cause.

The Fifth Amendment protects a citizen's rights during a trial. No one will stand trial unless a reasonable accusation has been made. No one can be tried twice for the same crime. Avoiding *self-incrimination* is also a citizen's right. The Fifth Amendment also prevents the

This 1919 poster, which features the Statue of Liberty, proclaims the advantages of living in America. Coming to the United States offers immigrants a better chance to "earn more, learn more" and even "own a home."

government from taking anyone's property unless it is in the public's best interest and a fair value is given for it.

The Sixth Amendment guarantees a speedy and public trial. It also ensures that a citizen has the right to know the charges he or she is being tried for and has the opportunity to confront witnesses and accusers.

The Seventh Amendment guarantees the right to a jury in a federal civil trial. The Eighth Amendment protects citizens against excessive *bail*, fines, and cruel and unusual punishments.

The Ninth Amendment protects any rights a citizen may have that aren't specifically written in the Constitution. Television, video games, and the Internet, for example, were not around when the Constitution was written in 1787. The Ninth Amendment extends already-written rights to issues concerning such modern-day inventions until the need arises to create new amendments.

The Tenth Amendment deals with the relationship between the states and the federal government. It says that any powers not assigned to the federal government belong to the states and their citizens.

Since the passage of the Bill of Rights, there have been 17 additional amendments. Not all of these amendments, however, concern citizenship. The Eleventh Amendment (passed in 1795) protects the states from certain types of lawsuits. The Twelfth Amendment (1804) sends the election of the president to the House of Representatives if the citizens and the Electoral College cannot come to a decision. The Seventeenth Amendment (1913) addresses *vacancies* in the Senate. The Twentieth Amendment (1933) sets the time period

UNITED STATES CONSTITUTION

For more than 200 years, the Constitution of the United States has been the supreme law of the country. It was written in 1787 at the Constitutional Convention in Philadelphia. The meeting was headed by George Washington and attended by 55 delegates representing 12 states (Rhode Island didn't send delegates). The first United States Congress added 12 amendments, but only 10 were agreed upon by the states. These 10 amendments are known today as the Bill of Rights. Besides George Washington, some other famous early Americans in attendance at the convention were Benjamin Franklin, James Madison, and Alexander Hamilton. Patrick Henry refused to attend, and Thomas Jefferson and John Adams were out of the country at the time. The original draft of the Constitution can be seen in the National Archives Building in Washington, D.C.

of a term of presidency and when Congressional sessions meet. The Twenty-second Amendment (1951) sets the number of terms for president at two (after Franklin D. Roosevelt was elected to four terms). The Twenty-fifth Amendment (1967) states that if the president resigns, the vice president takes office. And the Twenty-seventh Amendment (1992) addresses Congressional pay rates.

Certain other amendments deal directly with citizens' civil rights. The Thirteenth Amendment (1865) bans all slavery in the United States. The Fourteenth Amendment (1868) reinforces the Declaration of Independence's statement "that all men are created equal" by stating, "All persons born or naturalized in the United States...are citizens of the United States and the state wherein they reside." This

Visitors to the National Archives in Washington, D.C., look at original copies of the Declaration of Independence, the Constitution, and the Bill of Rights. These three documents are very important in American history, and great care is taken to make sure they are not damaged.

amendment also provides equal treatment to all citizens. The Fifteenth Amendment (1870) goes even further to say that no one can be denied the right to vote based on their race or on the fact that they were once slaves. The right to vote was extended to women with passage of the Nineteenth Amendment (1920). The Twenty-fourth Amendment (1964) restates that the right to vote is open to all citizens and addresses the issue of the *poll tax*. African Americans were being denied the right to vote unless they paid such a tax. The Twenty-sixth Amendment (1971) sets the voting age at 18.

The right to vote for the president of the United States is a basic American right, but it wasn't until the Twenty-third Amendment (1961) that residents of the District of Columbia were given this right.

Other amendments affect how citizens live. The Sixteenth Amendment (1913) allows Congress to impose an income tax. The Eighteenth Amendment (1919) started Prohibition, a ban on alcohol. It was later repealed by the Twenty-first Amendment (1933).

DECLARATION OF INDEPENDENCE

It took Thomas Jefferson and a committee of colonial leaders from June 11 to June 28, 1776, to write the Declaration of Independence. When it was finished, they had created a document that expressed the feelings of a new nation—a nation that embraced the freedoms and liberties of the individual. The Declaration of Independence also expressed the nation's outrage against the King of England:

> "He has obstructed the Administration of Justice
>
> For imposing Taxes on us without our consent
>
> For cutting off our Trade with all parts of the world
>
> He has plundered our seas, ravaged our Coasts, burnt our towns, and
>
> destroyed the lives of our people."

On July 4, 1776, such early Americans as John Hancock, Benjamin Franklin, John Adams, and Thomas Jefferson signed the Declaration of Independence. On that day, the United States of America was born. The original document can be seen in the rotunda of the National Archives Building in Washington, D.C.

Individuals take the Oath of Allegiance administered by a justice of the U.S. District Court at a swearing-in ceremony. The oath states that the person reciting it renounces any allegiance to a foreign country or power. Once the oath has been taken, these immigrants will be American citizens.

4

The first step an immigrant must take to gain U.S. citizenship is to get a United States Permanent Residence Card (also called a green card). This allows an immigrant to work and live in the United States permanently while seeking citizenship. Green cards are issued by U.S. Citizenship and Immigration Services (USCIS), the government agency that oversees immigration.

To get a green card, a person must apply to USCIS for a visa, a legal document that gives permission for that individual to enter the country. If the person already has an immediate relative—a spouse or children under the age of 18, for example—who are already U.S. citizens, their visa application is automatically approved. Otherwise, the immigrant must obtained a visa through the Diversity Visa Lottery, a program that was set up as part of the Immigration Act of 1990. The program is set up so that countries around the world do not continually receive *preferential* treatment year after year.

An immigrant can also acquire an employment-based visa. In this case, an employer applies to USCIS on behalf of the immigrant. If the visa is granted, the immigrant is expected to take the job.

Once an immigrant submits his or her visa application, he or she can get a temporary permit, the Employment Authorization Document, which permits the immigrant to work in the United States.

After five years, a permanent resident alien who wants to remain in the United States can apply for citizenship. The person has to meet certain requirements. These include being at least 18 years of age (children under 18 become citizens when their parents are naturalized), having a good moral character (for example, the person must have paid taxes and may not have been arrested for committing crimes), an ability to read and write the English language (unless the person is unable to do so for some physical reason, such as blindness), and having a knowledge of American history and its government.

As part of the citizenship application process, the immigrant must be photographed and fingerprinted. This data is submitted along with other paperwork required with the application.

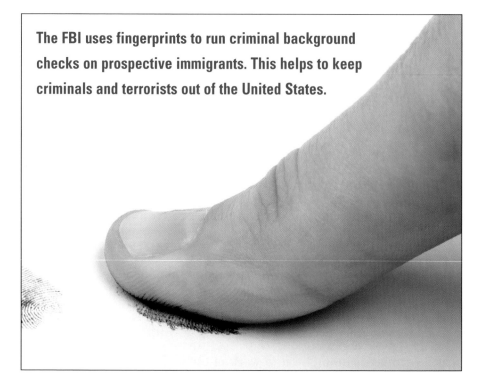

The FBI uses fingerprints to run criminal background checks on prospective immigrants. This helps to keep criminals and terrorists out of the United States.

CAN YOU PASS THE CITIZENSHIP TEST?

To become a naturalized U.S. citizen, immigrants have to take a test Some examples of the sentences that are dictated during the test are:

Red, white, and blue are the colors of the American flag.

The President lives in the White House.

As a citizen, I will be able to vote.

Some examples of questions on the multiple-choice test are:

Which document starts with "We the people of the United States":

A. Declaration of Independence

B. Constitution

C. Bill of Rights

D. First Amendment

The first line in the National Anthem is:

A. O say can you see

B. My country 'tis of thee

C. God Bless America

D. America, America

Just like any other test, studying is an important part in being able to pass. Before taking the test, immigrants are asked suggested subjects to study are:

- The discovery and settlement of the original 13 colonies
- Information about the Revolutionary War, the founding of the United States and its independence
- The Declaration of Independence, Constitution and its Amendments, including the Bill of Rights
- The history of the westward expansion
- Modern history (for example, women's rights, the Great Depression, World War II, the civil rights movement)
- Federal, state, and local government
- United States symbols (for example, the American Flag, Statue of Liberty, Liberty Bell, and Independence Hall)

Once U.S. Citizenship and Immigration Services receives the complete application, it schedules an interview for the prospective citizen. This is the next step in the naturalization process. During the interview, an immigration officer may ask the person to explain why he or she wanted to come to America. The officer will also ask the prospective citizen to explain anything about the application that is not clear.

During the interview, a citizenship test is given to determine the applicant's ability to read and write English and his or her knowledge of American history and government. The test consists of writing down on paper two **dictated** sentences, with at least one sentence written perfectly, and a knowledge test. The knowledge test can be given as an oral exam, but most people seeking citizenship prefer a multiple-choice test. A definite advantage to the multiple-choice test is being given a choice of answers. The test consists of 20 questions and takes about 30 minutes. Twelve correct answers are all that are needed to pass.

Sergei Khrushchev—son of a former premiere of the Soviet Union—reads a book entitled *A Welcome to U.S.A. Citizenship* as he waits to take the oath of allegiance to the United States to become a naturalized American citizen, 1999.

After the interview, the person will be notified whether USCIS will grant or deny the citizenship application. The government can also decide to continue the application, if the person has not provided all necessary information.

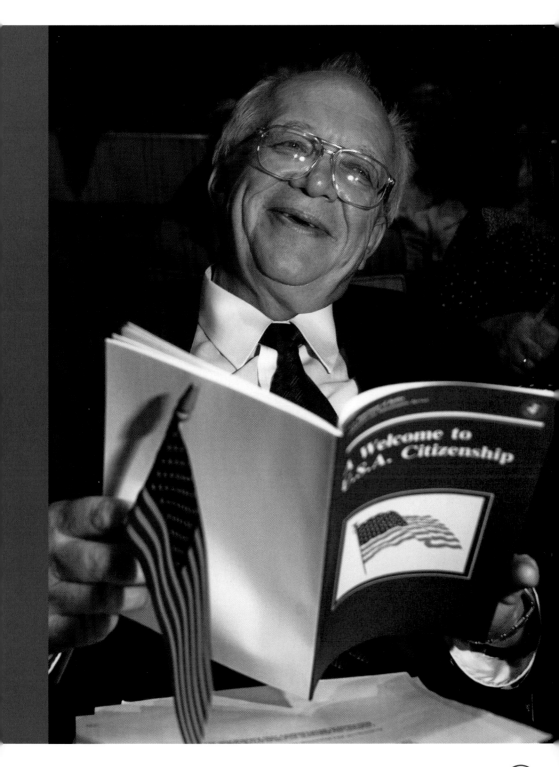

Across the country every day, students recite the pledge of allegiance to the American flag. This convention began in the late 19th century, after a man named Francis Bellamy wrote the oath and began a campaign to make it a morning tradition in schools throughout the country.

When USCIS approves an immigrant's citizenship application, that person is notified that he or she must appear at a naturalization ceremony. During this event, the immigrant will be required to take the Oath of Allegiance to the United States of America:

I hereby declare, on oath, that I absolutely and entirely renounce and abjure all allegiance and fidelity to any foreign prince, potentate, state, or sovereignty, of whom or which I have heretofore been a subject or citizen; that I will support and defend the Constitution and laws of the United States of America against all enemies, foreign and domestic; that I will bear true faith and allegiance to the same; that I will bear arms on behalf of the United States when required by the law; that I will perform noncombatant service in the armed forces of the United States when required by the law; that I will perform work of national importance under civilian direction when required by the law; and that I take this obligation freely without any mental reservation or purpose of evasion; so help me God.

By taking the oath, the new citizens pledges **allegiance** first and foremost to the United States. If an immigrant objects to the religious or military references in the oath, they can be omitted. Once a person has completed the naturalization ceremony, he or she is a full-fledged citizen of the United States. ✺

A husband and wife pose with their children, who were adopted from Korea. The passage of the Child Citizenship Act, which went into effect in 2001, has made it easier for children adopted from other countries to become U.S. citizens.

5 Immigration to the United States Today

On February 27, 2001, the Child Citizenship Act of 2000 went into effect. The act gave U.S. citizenship to children born outside the country if at least one parent is already a citizen. The child must be under 18, and it doesn't matter if the parent is a natural-born or naturalized citizen. For many American families adopting children from other countries, this was a great relief. It is estimated that 75,000 internationally adopted children have become citizens due to this act. Once the adoption is complete, the child is granted citizenship and all the rights and privileges that come with it.

The 2006 American Community Survey, a project of the U.S. Census Bureau, determined that the total population of the United States is more than 301 million. Today America is so diverse that the Census Bureau counts nearly 5 million people belonging to two or more racial categories.

In 2006, about 37.5 million people who had been born in another country were living in the United States. That's about 12.5 percent of the total population. According to Census Bureau data, 31 percent of the foreign-born residents are from Mexico, while 24 percent come from South and East Asia. Nearly 14 percent come from Central or South America, 9 percent from the Caribbean, and about 3 percent from the Middle East. The remaining 19 percent come from other

49

CENSUS

The U.S. Constitution requires that a census, or count of the population, be taken every ten years. This is a costly and time-consuming project. Today, census information is collected by mail, the Internet, and through personal interviews.

The questions asked in a census change as the population changes. Information collected in a census includes age, sex, ethnic background, marital status, and income. The information is collected to let the government and its officials know whom the citizens are in order to plan for beneficial public services, such as child-care centers, new roads and bridges, police and fire departments, elderly care, and schools. Businesses also use the information to plan for new factories, malls, and other services. In addition, the information is used to determine the number of seats a state gets in the House of Representatives and in the Electoral College. When a state gains or loses seats in the House or Electoral College, it is called reapportionment.

According to the U.S. Census Bureau, in 2008 the population of the United States is projected at more than 303 million.

Information about the most recent U.S. Census can be found on the Internet at www.census.gov.

A form for the 2000 U.S. Census arrives at a Missouri mailbox. The census forms were sent to more than 120 million U.S. households. They were used to gather data for the census, which takes place every ten years. The information collected by census workers is used to determine what programs will receive funding and what areas of the country need legislative or financial attention.

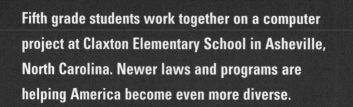

Fifth grade students work together on a computer project at Claxton Elementary School in Asheville, North Carolina. Newer laws and programs are helping America become even more diverse.

places, like Africa and Australia. About 35 percent of the foreign-born population have become naturalized citizens of the United States.

The fact that the United States has a high foreign-born population is nothing new. In 1850, as waves of Irish and German immigrants were coming to America, foreign-born Americans made up about 10 percent of the population. In 1910, at the height of a second great wave of immigration, about 15 percent of the U.S. population had been born in other countries. It is the continuous arrival of immigrants to America's shores that has made the United States the wonderful land of diversity that it is today. ✸

Chronology

c. 1000 Vikings land at L'Anse aux Meadows, Newfoundland; archaeological evidence suggests that a temporary settlement was established there.

1492 Christopher Columbus makes landfall in the Bahamas; his voyage opens the great era of European exploration and colonization in the New World.

1565 The Spanish establish St. Augustine; it is the oldest continuously inhabited European settlement in North America.

1607 Jamestown, Virginia, is established as the first permanent English settlement in North America.

1619 The first African-American slaves arrive in Virginia.

1620 Pilgrims seeking religious freedom land in Massachusetts and establish the Plymouth colony.

1775–83 The American Revolution is fought; immigration comes to a virtual standstill.

1796 Introduction of the Land Purchase Act; under the act, immigrants could buy 320 acres at $2 an acre.

1815 End of the Napoleonic Wars in Europe; beginning of European migration to America on a massive scale.

1861–65 Immigration to the United States comes to a virtual halt during the American Civil War, a bloody conflict between the Northern and Southern states.

1862 Adoption of the Homestead Act, which granted 160 acres of public land to a settler after a five-year occupancy; the Act helped settle the West.

1882 Adoption of the Chinese Exclusion Act.

1886 Installation and dedication of the Statue of Liberty, a gift from France, in New York Harbor.

1892 Establishment of Ellis Island immigration station; by the time it closes in 1954, more than 12 million immigrants will be processed at the station.

1921 Congress passes the Emergency Quota Act; this law imposes numerical limits on immigrants for the first time.

1924 The National Origins Act becomes America's first permanent immigration policy, imposing further limits on immigration along with national quotas.

1939-45 World War II; thousands of Jews, among other Europeans, flee the war and are allowed entry to America as refugees.

1965 The Immigration and Nationality Act abolishes the quota system based on national origin; the new system still imposes numerical limits, but has many exemptions.

1980 The Refugee Act sets a limit on the number of refugees who will be admitted to the United States in a particular year.

A section of a controversial wall being constructed along the U.S. border with Mexico, 2008. The wall is intended to prevent illegal border crossings and slow undocumented, or illegal, immigration from Mexico and Central America.

1986 The Immigration Reform and Control Act makes it illegal for employers to hire immigrants who have not entered the country legally.

1990 The Immigration Act increases the number of legal immigrants permitted to enter the United States each year; Ellis Island is re-opened as a museum.

1996 Illegal Immigration Reform and Immigrant Responsibility Act sets easier standards for deportation.

2001 The Child Citizenship Act, which gives citizenship to children born outside of the United States who have at least one citizen parent, goes into effect in February.

2003 The Immigration and Naturalization Service (INS) is dissolved; a new agency in the new Department of Homeland Security, Citizenship and Immigration Services, takes over most INS functions.

2005 The REAL ID Act permits the federal government to construct barriers at national borders. The law also places more restrictions on immigrants.

2007 The population of the United States is estimated to be 303 million. The population of Canada is estimated at 33.4 million.

2008 Activists protest against the construction of a security fence along the U.S. border with Mexico.

Glossary

Allegiance to support, to be loyal to, or to devote to a cause, leader, or country.

Allied joined by compact or treaty.

Amend to add or alter in some way.

Bail security given for the release of a prisoner.

Ban a legal or formal prohibition.

Census official account of a population's age, race, sex, income, and occupation.

Deportation lawfully sending someone back to his or her native country.

Dictate to speak or read for a person to write down or for a machine to record.

Dictatorship a form of government in which all power is held by one person or a small group.

Famine an extreme scarcity of food.

Multiple sclerosis a disease that affects the nerves and muscles.

Naturalize to undertake the process a person goes through to gain the rights and privileges of citizenship.

Persecution the act of harassing someone because of their beliefs.

Poll tax a tax of a fixed amount per person.

Preferential showing preference for.

Quota a number limit given to determine the amount of people allowed to immigrate to a country.

Self-incrimination the act of exposing oneself to prosecution.

Unconstitutional not according to or consistent with the constitution of a nation.

Vacancy an empty space.

Visa an official stamp on a passport allowing entry into the country giving the stamp.

Further Reading

Alesi, Gladys. *The U.S. Citizenship Test*. New York: Barron's Educational Series, 2008.

Bray, Ilona M., and Carl Falstrom. *U.S. Immigration Made Easy*. Berkeley, Calif.: NOLO, 2007.

Cieslik, Thomas, et al, editors. *Immigration: A Documentary and Reference Guide*. Westport, Conn.: Greenhaven Press, 2008.

Collier, C., and J.L. Collier. *A Century of Immigration, 1820–1924*. Tarrytown: Marshall Cavendish, 1999.

Freedman, Russell. *Immigrant Kids*. New York: Econo-Clad Books, 1999.

Hammerschmidt, Peter. *History of American Immigration*. Philadelphia: Mason Crest Publishers, 2009.

O'Donnell. *U.S. Immigration*. Mankato, Minn.: Capstone Press, 2008.

Schell, Richard, et al. *U.S. Immigration Citizenship Q&A*. Naperville, Ill.: Sphinx Publishing, 2008.

Internet Resources

http://www.census.gov

The official Web site of the U.S. Bureau of the Census contains information about the most recent census, taken in 2000.

http://www.ellisisland.org/

This Web site is devoted to the history of Ellis Island and the immigrants who came through its doors.

http://www.uscis.gov/portal/site/uscis

U.S. Citizenship and Immigration Services's official Web site provides information on becoming a citizen, one's rights and responsibilities, as well as forms, fees and other information.

http://www.archives.gov/index.html

This is the National Archives and Records Administration Web site, providing a place where people can conduct research on family members who immigrated to America.

http://www.usa.gov/

This Web site provides a tremendous amount of information on the United States government, its bodies and how well they work, as well as a breakdown of the government by topic.

http://www.usimmigrationsupport.org/

The United States Immigration Support organization is dedicated to guiding an immigrant through the naturalization/citizenship process.

Index

Photo Credits

Contributors

Barry Moreno has been librarian and historian at the Ellis Island Immigration Museum and the Statue of Liberty National Monument since 1988. He is the author of *The Statue of Liberty Encyclopedia,* which was published by Simon & Schuster in October 2000. He is a native of Los Angeles, California. After graduation from California State University at Los Angeles, where he earned a degree in history, he joined the National Park Service as a seasonal park ranger at the Statue of Liberty; he eventually became the monument's librarian. In his spare time, Barry enjoys reading, writing, and studying foreign languages and grammar. His biography has been included in *Who's Who Among Hispanic Americans, The Directory of National Park Service Historians, Who's Who in America,* and *The Directory of American Scholars.*

Rob Maury is currently working for a national magazine. His material has appeared in newspapers and on the Internet. He lives with his family in Hatfield, Pennsylvania.